Thomas Edison

A Photo-Illustrated Biography
by Greg Linder

Consultant:
Douglas Tarr
Reference Archivist
Edison National Historic Site

Bridgestone Books
an imprint of Capstone Press
Mankato, Minnesota

Bridgestone Books are published by Capstone Press
151 Good Counsel Drive, P.O. Box 669, Mankato, Minnesota 56002
http://www.capstone-press.com

Library of Congress Cataloging-in-Publication Data
Linder, Greg, 1950–
     Thomas Edison: a photo-illustrated biography/by Greg Linder.
     p. cm.—(photo-illustrated biographies)
     Includes bibliographical references and index.
     Summary: A biography of the man who invented the phonograph, the electric
lightbulb, and the motion picture and patented 1,093 inventions.
     ISBN 0-7368-0207-X
     1. Edison, Thomas A. (Thomas Alva), 1847–1931—Juvenile literature. 2. Edison, Thomas A.
(Thomas Alva), 1847–1931—Pictorial Works—Juvenile literature. 3. Inventors—United States—
Biography—Juvenile literature. [1. Edison, Thomas A. (Thomas Alva), 1847–1931. 2. Inventors.]
I. Title. II. Series.
TK140.E3L55 1999
621.3'092—dc21
[B]   98-31472
                                                                                                                  CIP
                                                                                                                  AC

J B
EDISON, T.A.

C. 1

Editorial Credits
Chuck Miller, editor; Timothy Halldin, cover designer; Kimberly Danger, photo researcher

Photo Credits
Corbis-Bettman, cover, 4, 6, 6 (inset), 8, 10, 12, 14, 16, 18, 20

2 3 4 5 6 04 03 02 01 00

Table of Contents

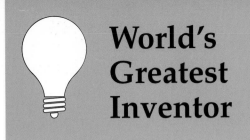

World's Greatest Inventor

Thomas Edison lived in an age of invention. People invented cars, airplanes, and the telephone during his lifetime. Many people consider Thomas the greatest inventor of his time.

Thomas received his first U.S. patent when he was 22 years old. A patent is an official piece of paper from the U.S. government. It prevents other people from copying and selling an invention.

Throughout his life, Thomas patented 1,093 different inventions. His most famous invention was the electric lightbulb. His phonograph led to the invention of stereos and compact disc players. Thomas was one of the first people to make movies with sound. He improved the telephone.

Thomas's inventions changed the world. Most of them are still in use today. Some people call Thomas the man who invented the future.

Thomas Edison spent much of his life in the laboratory. His hard work led to many inventions still used today.

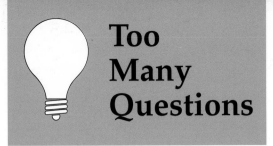

Too Many Questions

Thomas was born in Milan, Ohio, on February 11, 1847. He was the youngest of seven children.

Thomas's father, Samuel, sold timber and land. Thomas's mother, Nancy, was a teacher before Thomas was born.

The family moved to Port Huron, Michigan, when Thomas was seven. He started school in 1855. The schoolmaster thought Thomas asked too many questions. He thought Thomas could not learn in a school classroom.

Nancy took Thomas out of school after just three months. She taught him at home and gave him books to read. Some of the books were about science experiments. Thomas set up a laboratory in his family's basement. He worked on many different experiments in the laboratory. Samuel said Thomas spent most of his time in the basement.

Thomas's childhood home still stands in Milan, Ohio. Visitors tour the house and see the room where Thomas was born.

A Boy in Business

In 1859, the Grand Trunk Railroad came to Port Huron. Thomas took a job as a news butch at the age of 12. He sold newspapers, magazines, and candy on the train.

At age 15, Thomas bought an old printing press. He set up the machine in a railroad car. He wrote and printed his own newspaper. Thomas sold copies of the newspaper for eight cents each.

One day in 1862, Thomas was selling papers at the railway station. He saw a boxcar rolling toward the stationmaster's two-year-old son. Thomas leaped onto the tracks and saved him.

As a reward, the stationmaster taught Thomas to use the station's telegraph. This machine sent Morse code messages over electric wires. In Morse code, dots and dashes stand for letters. Thomas worked as a telegraph operator for the next seven years.

Thomas began to travel the United States as a telegraph operator at age 15. He worked mainly for the Western Union Company.

"I'll never give up. I may have a streak of luck before I die."
—*To a friend, July 26, 1869*

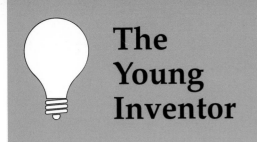

The Young Inventor

In 1868, Thomas moved to Boston. He worked as a telegraph operator there. Much of the time, he had no messages to receive or send. Thomas had time to work on his experiments and inventions.

Thomas finished his first invention in 1869. He made a machine that automatically counted votes. But no one wanted to buy his machine. Thomas did not give up inventing. He quit his job as a telegraph operator to be a full-time inventor.

Thomas's next invention was an improved stock ticker. A stock ticker prints current prices from the stock market. Someone who owns a stock owns part of a company. Thomas's stock ticker was the first to print words as well as numbers.

Thomas's first big success came in 1870. He sold one of his stock tickers to the Western Union Company for $40,000.

Thomas made many improvements to the telegraph in the 1870s. He found a way to send and receive four messages at once.

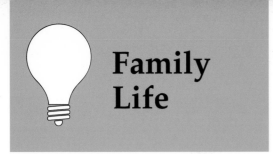

Family Life

Thomas married Mary Stilwell in 1871. She and Thomas worked for the same telegraph company.

Mary and Thomas had three children. They were Marion, Thomas Junior, and William. Thomas had nicknames for Marion and Thomas Jr. He called them Dot and Dash. The names came from his work with the telegraph and Morse code.

In 1884, Mary Edison caught an illness. She died at age 29.

Thomas married Mina Miller in 1886. They had three children. Their names were Madeleine, Charles, and Theodore.

Thomas and Mina were married for 45 years. In later years, Thomas became almost deaf. Mina helped him understand what people were saying. She would tap their words on Thomas's knee in Morse code.

Thomas married his second wife, Mina, in 1886. Theodore and Madeleine were two of Thomas's six children.

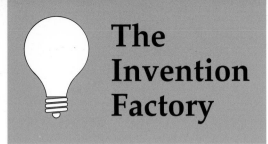

The Invention Factory

In 1876, Thomas built a large laboratory in Menlo Park, New Jersey. The laboratory was the world's first invention factory. Tools, chemicals, and science books filled the laboratory.

Some people think this laboratory was Thomas's most important idea. Thomas and his assistants worked only on inventions. Thomas worked 18 hours a day for much of his life. He sometimes even slept at the laboratory.

Thomas wanted to improve a new machine called the telephone. Alexander Graham Bell invented the telephone in 1876. People had trouble hearing each other on Alexander's telephone.

In 1877, Thomas invented a new telephone transmitter. A transmitter turns sound into an electrical signal. People could hear voices louder and clearer with Thomas's transmitter.

Thomas (seated on the far right) and his assistants worked long hours. Many days, they ate and slept in the laboratory.

"Genius is one percent inspiration and 99 percent perspiration."
–One of Thomas's favorite sayings. He repeated it often.

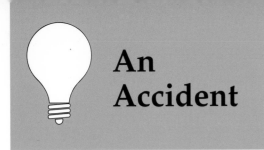

An Accident

In 1877, Thomas created one of his most famous inventions by accident. He was working on a way to record telegraph messages. He invented the phonograph, or record player.

The first words ever heard on the phonograph were from a nursery rhyme. Laboratory workers heard Thomas reciting "Mary Had a Little Lamb."

Thomas improved the phonograph during the next 20 years. He even invented a talking doll. Thomas placed a small phonograph inside the doll. Children turned a crank to make the phonograph play. It sounded as if the doll was talking.

Many people could not believe Thomas was able to record a human voice. Thomas now had a nickname. People began calling him the Wizard of Menlo Park.

Thomas did not give up easily. He worked for days without rest to build an early phonograph.

glass bulb

filament

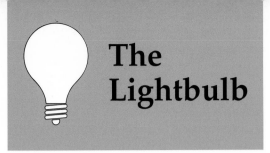

The Lightbulb

In 1878, people lit their homes with gas lights, candles, or oil lamps. The lights were dim and often caused fires.

Thomas wanted to make a bright light that was safe to use indoors. He started with a glass bulb. He removed the air from the bulb with a vacuum. He placed a filament inside. A filament is a thin wire or thread. Thomas ran electricity through the filament.

At first, the filaments burned up quickly and fell apart. Thomas and his assistants worked for months. They tested thousands of filaments. They used many kinds of wires and threads.

In 1879, Thomas tested a filament made from carbonized sewing thread. Carbonized means partly burned. The bulb glowed for 13 hours. It was the first successful lightbulb. By 1900, millions of people were using Thomas's electric lightbulbs.

Thomas and his assistants tested thousands of kinds of filaments. They chose carbonized thread because it did not burn up.

"A large part of education in coming generations will not be by books, but by moving pictures. I have tried this out in experimenting with children, and the results have been astonishing. Children don't need many books when they are shown how to do things."
–Thomas to composer John Philip Sousa, October 1923

Later Years

In 1888, Thomas invented the kinetoscope. This machine was a wooden box with a strip of film inside. Viewers looked through a small hole to see the film move. These strips of film in the box were the world's first movies.

In 1914, Thomas combined the kinetoscope and the phonograph. He showed a movie on a screen. He ran the phonograph at the same time. He had combined a movie with sound.

Thomas never stopped inventing. He invented an electric railway and an electric pen. He invented a new way to mine iron ore.

Thomas died on October 18, 1931. People remember him as a master of light, sound, and electricity. He was a man of ideas who would not give up. Many people think Thomas was the greatest inventor of his time.

Thomas's kinetoscope led to the invention of movie projectors. Movie projectors allowed movies to be shown in theaters.

Fast Facts about Thomas Edison

 Thomas often liked to work in the laboratory all night.
He would go home in the morning and sleep most of the day.

 Thomas proposed marriage to his second wife with Morse code.
He tapped out the proposal on Mina's hand.

 Thomas patented his first invention in 1869. His last invention
was patented in 1933, two years after his death.

Important Dates in Thomas Edison's Life

1847—Born February 11 in Milan, Ohio

1869—Receives a patent on a machine that counts votes

1871—Marries Mary Stilwell

1876—Starts world's first invention factory in Menlo Park, New Jersey

1877—Invents the phonograph and a new transmitter for the telephone

1879—Tests the first successful electric lightbulb

1886—Marries Mina Miller

1888—Invents the kinetoscope

1931—Dies on October 18 in West Orange, New Jersey

Words to Know

carbonized (KAR-buhn-ized)—partly burned

filament (FIL-uh-muhnt)—a thin wire or thread; Thomas used a filament in the electric light bulb.

invent (in-VEHNT)—to create a new thing or method

laboratory (LAB-ruh-tor-ee)—a place where people do experiments

Morse code (MORSS-KODE)—a system of dots and dashes used by telegraph operators to send messages over electric wires

patent (PAT-uhnt)—an official piece of paper from the U.S. government; a patent prevents anyone from copying and selling an invention.

stock market (STOCK MAHR-kit)—a place where stocks are bought and sold; someone who owns a stock owns part of a company.

Read More

Adair, Gene. *Thomas Alva Edison: Inventing the Electric Age.* Oxford Portraits in Science. New York: Oxford University Press, 1996.

Bedik, Shelley. *Thomas Edison, Great American Inventor.* New York: Scholastic, 1995.

Parker, Steve. *Thomas Edison and Electricity.* New York: Chelsea House, 1995.

Useful Addresses

The Edison National Historic Site
Main Street and Lakeside Avenue
West Orange, NJ 07052

**Thomas Edison
Birthplace Museum**
9 Edison Drive
Box 451
Milan, OH 44846

Internet Sites

Edison National Historic Site
http://www.nps.gov/edis/home.htm
The National Inventors Hall of Fame
http://www.invent.org/book/index.html
Super Scientists
http://www.energy.ca.gov/education/scientists/index.html#return

Index